journey to purpose

a journey worth taking

·nichole chavez·

EQUIP PRESS

Colorado Springs

journey to
purpose

Journey to Purpose
Copyright © 2018 by Nichole Chavez

Published by Equip Press
5550 Tech Center Drive
Colorado Springs, CO 80919

Printed in the United States of America

First Edition: 2018
Journey to Purpose / Nichole Chavez
Paperback ISBN: 978-1-946453-45-7
eBook ISBN: 978-1-946453-46-4

a note from nichole

Purpose is one of the most difficult non-tangibles to grasp, much less write about. But since I have doubted the existence of purpose, wrestled with purpose, fought against purpose, and denied purpose at various points in my life, who better to write about purpose than someone who has accepted it and then embraced it wholeheartedly.

My journey was not easy. And it still isn't. There is so much fear, insecurity, self-doubt, and emotion that comes along with acknowledging, accepting, stepping into, and living my purpose. The enemy used these things against me to cloud my vision. I could not see past my negative emotions to the point that I could neither accept nor live out my purpose.

It wasn't until I started to accept who I am in Christ that I started a journey to purpose. I didn't hop straight to it, and it didn't magically appear. Before I began to see my purpose, I had to go through a process of trust, love, and obedience to God. Then I had to build a relationship with Jesus. As I did that, His purpose became a little bit clearer. It started to burn in my soul and it spurred me to action. It was my relationship with Jesus that revealed my purpose, it was trust in Jesus that helped me accept my purpose, and it was faith in Jesus that made me step into my purpose.

Everyone's journey to and through purpose is different. Our journeys are as different as our fingerprints. The only constant and the only thing we all have in common is Jesus. He is the constant, never-changing, ever-present, inspirational purpose-giver in our lives. Because He never changes, we can confidently learn from each other because it is Him who teaches us all.

We will be going through a journey of purpose, we will learn from some of the widely known Bible heroes and some of the unknown, unrecognizable heroes. Together we will learn what God says about us and what He is saying to us about our purpose.

Journey to Purpose is just that; it's a personal journey through and to purpose. There are no right or wrong answers, no super hard spiritual questions. Answer honestly and you will find your way to purpose, you will find what has been holding you back, and you will find your way forward.

I designed this study to be done with a friend, a group of friends, or after going on this journey together, we are now friends group. The journey to purpose can be a long and hard one, but it can be so much easier with the help of others who are on the same journey. If you are embarking on this expedition with just your hot cup of something and a pen, that's ok too, enjoy the journey, share your progress, struggles and victories with someone, bring them on your journey to purpose.

You are stepping into a six-week journey. Each week will be started with your group and will be followed by three days of solo exploration. What are you supposed to do with the remaining days, you ask? You reflect, you pray, you act, you self-examine, you read the Bible verses I am referencing in that week's study over and over again, and you can share this study with someone who needs to set out on this journey as well. You get to decide how you spend the days in between, but you don't get to quit.

I pray that God speaks to you and opens your eyes to the purpose He has for you, I pray that your journey blesses you and those around you, but most importantly, I pray that this journey leads you to the heart of God.

So grab a warm cup of something and get ready. We are about to embark on the journey of a lifetime full of purpose.

hidden purpose

do I have a purpose

Let's start by talking about your elusive, scary, small, insignificant, big, spectacular, ordinary, or special purpose.

Circle the descriptive word above that you think best describes your purpose.

Do you have a God-given purpose? Are you sure? How do you know?

To be confident in your purpose, you have to be confident in the answers above. No matter what your answer is, we can always grow. And that is what we will do together over the next six weeks.

The best place to start is at the beginning and with honesty. If you don't know if you have a purpose, then answer, "I don't know." If you think you had a purpose in the past but you can't see it now, then write that down. Write down the first thing that pops into your head.

Let's try again.

Do you have a God-given purpose? Are you sure? How do you know?

Which scripture do you go to that will back up your claim to purpose? Don't know? Find one together.

Why must you have a scripture to back you up?

The enemy is out to diminish any impact you will have when you step into your purpose. He wants to stop you in your tracks. And if you are not certain what God says about you and what God is trying to say to you, then you can be stopped. But if you are rock solid on who God made you and why He made you, you are an unstoppable force for God.

From one moment to the next, our confidence in our purpose can be shaken. But if you know that God has brought you into this world for a purpose, then knowing what your purpose is isn't as important as knowing you have one.

Let's read that again.

If you know that God has brought you into this world for a purpose, then knowing what your purpose is isn't as important as knowing you have one. In other words, it is more important to know you have a purpose than it is to know precisely what that purpose is.

Often, our purpose is drawn out and lived out, hiding in the busyness of our day and lives. Sometimes we can only see it in the rearview mirror, and other times we see it far off in the distance.

Faith in God's master plan for you will keep you going in the dry seasons, and faith will keep you afloat when the rains come flooding in.

So, if you are unsure what your purpose is, that's okay. God assures you that you have one. By the end of this study, I hope you will feel confident that His purpose is good. His purpose is tailor-made for you and woven into the fabric of your life to be lived out by you and enjoyed by God.

Look these scriptures up together and write them down.

Psalm 139:13-16

Ephesians 2:10

You were created for GOOD WORKS, which God prepared beforehand just for you so that you will accomplish them. You have a purpose and it is good.

hidden purpose

Eve

The very first woman to grace this planet was made with a purpose. Even though she sinned, she continued on with her purpose until the day she took her last breath.

Read Genesis Chapter 2. Write the verse that references Eve's God-appointed purpose below.

Some ladies are uncomfortable with the fact that Eve's purpose was to be a helper to Adam. But Eve was not uncomfortable with her purpose — the Bible never says Eve didn't enjoy or didn't like her role as Adam's helper. God put a purpose in her and she lived it. He wove that purpose into the fabric of her being when He created her. Her purpose was as fixed as her height or eye color. She wasn't resentful of it or afraid of it. She lived it because that is what God created her to be and do.

Being able to read about the creation of Eve is like watching our own creation. He created her just as He created us, leaving nothing out. He created us with a purpose, just like he made Eve with a purpose. He didn't just mix us up and throw us out there and say: "Well, let's see what this one does". Whatever she figures out she's good at, that will be her purpose."

He thought about you, planned you, and knit you together in your mother's womb. You were fearfully and wonderfully made to change the world around you with the purpose He put inside of you.

Eve's sin in the Garden of Eden has defined her in our minds since day one. But her sin did not define her in God's mind. He forgave her, and she continued to live out her purpose.

Has your sin defined you in your mind?

Eve sinned and continued living. She lived with the consequences of her sin all while living out her purpose. If you think your sin cancels out your purpose, all you have to do is read the Bible to find out that it does not! The Bible is full of people who sinned and still lived out the purpose God put inside of them. The key was repentance.

Do you feel like your past has canceled out your purpose? Why?

Do you feel like you don't deserve to have a purpose because of your sin? Why?

In many ways, Eve's life doesn't look like it should be the first example of a life of purpose lived out. Her mistake is widely known throughout the world. Her sin has literally gone viral for thousands of years.

How is she the first example of purpose lived out?

Her sin and mistakes did not change the purpose God planned for her life. Purpose is not given or taken away because of our sin. Like salvation and forgiveness, purpose is a free gift to all who will receive it and embrace it.

"For we are God's workmanship, created in Christ Jesus to do good works, which God prepared in advance <u>as our way of life</u>" (Ephesians 2:10 BSB).

Read that verse out loud. Now fill in the blanks.

_____ (insert your name) is God's _____ , created in Christ Jesus to do _____ .

God prepared this and _____ (insert your name) in _____ .

As _____ (insert your name) way of life.

Isn't it beautiful when you put your name on His promises? Isn't it reassuring to know that God has prepared you to do "good works" and live out your purpose just by being the person God created you to be!

His plan depends on your acceptance and acknowledgment of His purpose for your life. His plan and purpose depend on you knowing just how precious and special you are to Him.

You may not be able to see how God can use you after your brokenness, hurt, bitterness, un-forgiveness, addiction, unfaithfulness, and sinfulness. But God sees a lady who He created on purpose and for a purpose.

If you know that God has brought you into this world for a purpose, then knowing what your purpose is isn't as important as knowing you have one.

hidden purpose

Sarah

We have learned that sin doesn't change or take away the purpose God has given us. Our purpose is a free gift from God to us, to be used by us for Him.

There is a lady in the Bible named Sarah. She received a promise directly from God himself that she would give birth to a son, and that son would be the beginning of a lineage that makes the pedigree of the English monarchy laughable. She would give birth not just to a son, but also to a nation.

Read Genesis 16:1-6, 17:15-19

Did Sarah see in Chapter 16 the plan God had in Chapter 17? Why not?

What do you think was going through Sarah's mind when she told Abraham to sleep with her servant?

God is not required to reveal His plan to you. Your faith requires you to believe that He has a plan and purpose for you even if you can't see it.

> Then one of them (an angel) said, "I will return to you about this time next year, and your wife, Sarah, will have a son."
>
> Sarah was listening to this conversation from the tent. Abraham and Sarah were both very old by this time, and Sarah was long past the age of having children.
>
> So she laughed silently to herself and said, "How could a worn-out woman like me enjoy such pleasure, especially when my master—my husband—is also so old?"
>
> Then the LORD said to Abraham, "Why did Sarah laugh? Why did she say, 'Can an old woman like me have a baby?' "Is anything too hard for the LORD? I will return about this time next year, and Sarah will have a son."
>
> Sarah was afraid, so she denied it, saying, "I didn't laugh."
>
> But the LORD said, "No, you did laugh." (Genesis 18:10-15 NLT)

Can you imagine being called out by God because you laughed at His promise and His plan?

Have you laughed, smirked, or doubted that God has given you a purpose? Why?

That is exactly what Sarah did. She laughed because she couldn't see how God could possibly make good on His promise. She had lived a whole life waiting, making mistake after mistake, trying to make it happen. She tried her own way. She tried forcing a solution. She tried giving up. She made a mess of things, but that didn't change God's mind about His plan and her purpose.

Write out Genesis 21:1-3 below

I love verse two, "This happened at just the time God had said it would." He kept His word! He did for Sarah what He had promised. He will do the same for you. He says He created each and every one of us with a purpose, and He will fulfill His promise in each and every one of us if we let Him.

I wish we came with instructions. I wish God could tell each of us, "You will be this age when I decide to use you in this way to change this part of the world and this is how you will do it." God knows when your purpose will be revealed, when it will be used, and for what purpose. Our faith requires us to trust that it will happen at just the time God says it will.

Sarah wasn't confident that God had a plan. Are you confident that God has a plan for you? "For I know the plans I have for you," says the LORD.

"They are plans for good and not for disaster, to give you a future and a hope" (Jeremiah 29:11 NLT). God says he knows the plans He has for you. They are good and they are for your good.

Fill in the blanks:

For I know that God has plans for _____ (insert your name). They are plans for _____ and not for _____ . They will be my _____ and they will be full of _____ .

If you know that God has brought you into this world for a purpose, then knowing what your purpose is isn't as important as knowing you have one.

hidden purpose

David

God's plan depends on your acceptance and acknowledgment of His purpose for your life. It depends on you knowing just how precious and special you are to God.

Do you know how precious you are to God? Write down one word God would use to describe you. Write down one word you would use to describe yourself.

David knew exactly how precious he was to God. We read just how secure David was in his relationship with God and how very precious he knew he was in Psalm 139.

Read this prayer to God.

Psalm 139:13-16
> *You made all the delicate, inner parts of my body*
> *and knit me together in my mother's womb.*
> *Thank you for making me so wonderfully complex!*
> *Your workmanship is marvelous — how well I know it.*
> *You watched me as I was being formed in utter seclusion,*
> *as I was woven together in the dark of the womb.*

You saw me before I was born.
Every day of my life was recorded in your book.
Every moment was laid out
before a single day had passed.

How precious are your thoughts about me, O God.
They cannot be numbered!
I can't even count them;
they outnumber the grains of sand!
And when I wake up,
you are still with me. (NLT)

This was David's prayer to God; for some reason, for all these years, I thought it was God talking to David. The confidence shown here is almost unrecognizable from a human being. The words he chose to use when describing how God thought about him are inspiring, humbling, and amazing! David was able to see himself through God's eyes.

Where did he get that kind of confidence?

Do you have that kind of confidence?

Have you ever thanked God for making you so wonderfully complex? I might describe myself as complex, but wonderfully complex? Probably not. That would take way too much self-awareness, an acceptance of our humanity, and acknowledgment that God made us that way. David is oozing acceptance of who he is and the fact that God made him. He is accepting that God didn't accidentally put him on this earth and then need to figure out what to do with him.

David talks about his own creation the way we would talk about the creation of our world: with wonder and amazement. David is in awe of the way God meticulously created him. Then David goes a step further and compliments God with the words "your workmanship is marvelous."

Conceited much, David? But in fact, it wasn't conceit. It was an acknowledgment that God is perfect and His workmanship is beautiful. If David accepts and acknowledges the beauty of God's creation of the world, the universe, and everything in it, David must also acknowledge the beauty in the creation of himself.

Think about that for a moment. *If David accepts and acknowledges the beauty of God's creation of the world, the universe, and everything in it, David must also acknowledge the beauty in the creation of himself.*

Do you think God created an amazing world?

Do you think He created an amazing person when He created you? When answering this question, don't look through the lens of your past or present or what you have done or has been done to you. Look at yourself through the lens of God's love for you. Then answer the question.

David takes his acknowledgment a step further by understanding he cannot leave anything out of his prayers of thankfulness. He must thank God for his own creation because it is good!

Your life was not an accident. You have not been forgotten or overlooked. Your present circumstances are temporary and are not dismissed by God. He does not define you by your circumstances or dismiss you because of them.

David says, "How precious are your thoughts about me, O God. They cannot be numbered! I can't even count them; they outnumber the grains of sand!

And when I wake up, you are still with me!"

Pray David's prayer. Thank God for making you. Thank Him for the complex person that you are. Tell Him that His workmanship is marvelous. Thank Him for laying out every moment of your life. Acknowledge that even if your life isn't going the way you want it to or think it should go; God still has a purpose planned for your life.

Accept yourself for who God sees you to be. He thinks precious thoughts about you, so many that they can't even be counted. They outnumber the grains of sand. When you fall asleep, He is with you. And when you wake up, He is still there.

You are a masterpiece, wonderfully complex and marvelous. You were created on purpose and with a purpose and loved by God Himself!

Write out Psalm 139:13-16 and insert your name in the passage. When you are done writing it out, say it out loud until it doesn't get stuck in your throat. Speak the words until you can say them with the same confidence David did. God wants us to see ourselves the way He sees us.

If you know that God has brought you into this world for a purpose, then knowing what your purpose is isn't as important as knowing you have one.

disguised purpose

hidden purpose

You know God created you lovingly and you know He loves you. You know you were created with a purpose, for a purpose, and on purpose. You are in God's thoughts when you fall asleep and He is there with you when you wake up. You are a masterpiece, wonderfully complex and marvelous. You know that God has woven His purpose for your life into the fabric of your being when He created you.

We have also learned that knowing that God has brought you into the world for a purpose and knowing that you have a purpose is more important than knowing what your purpose is.

Eventually, we would all like to know what our purpose is, right? That is the whole goal of studies like this. Can I tell you what it is? No. Only God knows what He has planned for you and what purpose He has put inside of you.

After accepting the fact that He has a plan for you is, the next step is to trust He will work it through you.

Do you believe He is working His plan through you?

In what ways do you see His plan at work?

If you can't see His plan at work in your life, that's ok. You are not alone, and you are in good company. Esther had the same problem. She couldn't see what purpose she played in God's plan until it was over. She had to trust God. She had to trust that He was working His purpose through her even if she didn't see it. She had been through so much loss and so much pain that her purpose was buried under hurt, fear, and grief.

Maybe you have been through a period of your life when you knew you were living out your purpose. But then life changed, mistakes were made, and you suddenly found yourself adrift, hoping to get back what was lost. In times like these, your purpose is not lost. It is merely disguised, hiding in plain sight.

What is your purpose disguised as? What is your purpose hiding behind?
Fear, Hurt, Loss, Insecurity, Unworthiness, Your Past, Your Present, Life

Sometimes it is easy to lose sight of purpose because all you can see is the pain of the past and the present. You can't imagine how your purpose and this life can be compatible._

You may be asking yourself "How can God look at my life and still see purpose in it?!"

> "I will seek the lost, and I will bring back the strayed, and I will bind up the injured, and I will strengthen the weak..." (Ezekiel 34:16 ESV).

Feeling lost? He will look for you. Have you strayed away? He will bring you back. Are you injured? He will bind up your wounds. Are you weak? He will give you strength. Your present circumstances have nothing to do with God's ability to work His purpose through you. He promises to find you if you wander off, He promises to bind up your wounds if you are injured, and He will give you strength if you are weak.

He has a solution for every problem, He didn't bring you into this world only to leave you to fend for yourself. He planned on being there with you every step of the way, lighting your path along the way.

Look up and write down Psalm 119:105

Over the next few days you are going to learn about Esther and her disguised, discouraging, bumpy, hurtful, dangerous, and scary road to purpose. She had no idea that her purpose was on the other side of so much loss and pain. Her purpose was hidden in the details of her life. There was no way for her to ever know what was to come or that her trust in God would be critical to her fulfillment of her purpose. She had one choice and one choice only. Esther had to know to trust in the Lord with all her heart, to know that He is for her and not against her, to know that He has a plan and it is not to harm her, and, above all else, to know that He loves her.

He loves you and He will light your path. He will guide your steps. He will fulfill His plan, and you will fulfill your purpose.

disguised purpose

Esther

Esther's purpose was initially buried underneath heartache, loss, and confusion. The Bible gives us a look at her life after it is all said and done, but she lived it — she lived every excruciating moment of it — without a hint of the purpose her future held. As we read through the story of her life, we will see that she never once said, "this must be my purpose" or "oh, so this is the plan." She was as much in the dark as we are with our lives and purpose.

I'm sure she never saw herself as part of God's plan. I'm sure she never saw what was to come as part of her purpose.

If you can't see His plan at work in your life, that's ok. You are not alone.

Esther never had a direct encounter with God. Her story was designed, orchestrated, and protected by God, but His obvious direction is nowhere to be found in the book of Esther. This story tells us that not everyone needs to hear exact next steps spelled out directly from the mouth of God to make a difference or to live out their purpose.

Esther had a sad start to her life. She could have easily seen herself as an outsider, she could have felt her life was without purpose, or she could have even have perceived herself to be forgotten by God.

Read Esther Chapter 2:5-7

What brought Mordecai to Susa?

How did Esther end up with Mordecai?

Mordecai was in Susa because he was brought there as a captive, and Esther was living with Mordecai because her parents died. This does not sound much like the beginning of a purposeful life, does it? Most of us struggle to see God's hand and God's purpose in lives filled with suffering, sadness, and struggle. Nevertheless, God created Esther for a purpose. No matter her life circumstances, she was going to live His plan and live her purpose because God envisioned it, He orchestrated it, and He protected it.

But before she can live His plan and purpose, her world gets turned upside down.

Has your world ever been turned upside down?

Do you see it as the end — or perhaps the beginning — of your purpose? Do you see that life event as part of your purpose?

In Chapter One of the book of Esther, we read about a king named Xerxes and his wife, Queen Vashti. In this chapter they have an epic fight that results in Xerxes banishing Vashti. The King is suddenly in search of a new queen.

This is where Esther enters the scene. She is taken from her family and added to a harem of women from which King Xerxes will choose his next wife. How many women do you think she knew saved a nation after being added to a harem?

Do you see your past or present situation as an impossible platform for an amazing purpose?

Read Esther 2:8

The NIV version of this scripture says she was *"taken to the king's palace."* The word "taken" stood out to me. I can't image Esther went happily. She was taken from the life she knew, she was taken from her family, and she was taken from her planned future. Everything she had spent her life dreaming and hoping for was suddenly taken away.

Do you feel like parts of your life have been taken away from you? What was taken?

Do you feel you can never get back what was taken? Why?

Do you feel angry, upset, depressed or sad about it? Why?

Sometimes we are taken from what is safe and good in our lives and thrown into a situation that is hurtful, damaging, or scary and we can't see how God can use the situation. If we are honest, we don't want to think about how God can use the situation because the situation is too big or too hurtful to see past. But no situation is too big or hurtful for God. He sees those big, hurtful things in our lives as opportunities to do big healing and work big miracles. He knows each of us can accomplish our purpose in a big way, in spite of whatever has been taken.

> "For I know the plans I have for you," says the LORD. "They are plans for good and not for disaster, to give you a future and a hope" (Jeremiah 29:11 NLT).

Fill in the blanks:

For I know that God has plans for _____ (insert your name). They are plans for _____ and not for _____ . They will be my _____ and they will be full of _____ .

He knows the plans HE has for you. It doesn't matter what anybody else has planned for you, has done to you, or what has happened around you. If you say "yes" to His plan for your life, He will give you a future. There is so much hope in that.

disguised purpose

Esther

Esther was not hidden from God while she was in the harem. She was not sheltered from His presence and she wasn't cut off from His purpose for her life. God used the hatred, lies, and sin of others to fulfill His plan for her life. Let me make this perfectly clear: God did not *cause* the sin to fulfill His purpose; rather, He *used* the sin to fulfill His purpose.

Read and write down Romans 8:28

All things work together for good. ALL THINGS. That means Jesus takes it ALL — things that are good, bad, hurtful, painful, happy, sad, devastating, unforgivable — and weaves them together for good. He weaves them together with threads of grace and forgiveness, healing and restoration. He leaves no part of your life untouched. He takes your life as a whole and uses it for His purpose and your good. All those things in your life that you are ashamed of, all those mistakes and missteps, all those things done to you or caused by you. He takes all of them and works them together for good. Isn't God amazing?

If you love God, you can't outrun, out-sin, out-hurt, or outlive your purpose, because it is a purpose given to you. Your purpose is protected and inspired by God.

Do you believe that God can and will take the entirety of your past and present and work it together for your good and His purpose? Why or why not?

Esther finds herself in favor with King Xerxes, and before she knows it she is queen. If the life I knew before was taken from me, then there's only one thing that could make it up to me … making me a queen, right? I might not complain after the crown is put on my head — I mean, who doesn't want to become a queen or at the very least own a crown?

For Esther, becoming queen may have felt like relief. It may have felt like things were finally falling into place. She may have felt peace in her new circumstances. But her life wasn't over, her purpose was still in play, and God's plan had yet to be completed in her life. She was going to need all the strength, trust, and faith she could muster in order for the sin of Haman to be worked for her good and the good of a nation.

What would it take for you to look at your life, both past and present, and truly believe that God will work it all out for your good and His purpose?

What would change in your heart and in your relationship with Jesus if you looked at attacks against you — lies, betrayal, anger, jealousy, adultery, and sin — as experiences that are about to be worked together for your good?

Read Esther Chapter Three

Esther's life is about to be turned upside down again, this time by the jealousy, hatred, and pride of Haman. But little does Haman know that he is actually setting the stage upon which Esther will fulfill her purpose. Haman sets the stage for God to fulfill His plan.

Do you feel like Esther? Has your life has been turned upside down by the sin of others? Because of their sin, has your life has been hard and full of hurt? You may feel as though God has forgotten about you. You may feel He has left you to fend for yourself and you are tired of fighting.

Would the fight be worth it if you knew that God was going to turn it around for good?

Romans 8:28 NLT (insert your name):

And _____ knows that God causes everything to work together for the good of _____ , who loves God and is called according to His purpose for _____ .

If you know that God has brought you into this world for a purpose, then knowing what your purpose is isn't as important as knowing you have one. In time you will find that God was working His plan and your purpose through you all along.

disguised purpose

Esther

Esther gets word that her people, the Jews, are on the verge of being annihilated — completely wiped out of existence — and the only thing that is standing between her people and death is her. Esther alone can save them. No pressure, right?

Read Esther Chapter Four. Write out the scriptures that speak to you. Why do they speak to you?

Esther has a choice to make in this chapter, doesn't she? Esther has no idea what the outcome will be if she goes to the king with the news that she is a Jew. Her people are about to be killed; she has no idea if this boldness to step into her purpose will end her life, too. We know the end of the story, but Esther does not. She is living every exhausting, painful, and excruciating moment of it.

Sound familiar? We are doing the same exact thing. We are living out our lives moment by moment. We can only see what has already happened and what is happening at this exact moment. The future is a mystery known only to God. Then, one day, we run right into purpose.

Would you recognize it if it was happening to you right now?

Esther didn't immediately see her purpose. She was as human as we are, and she was afraid. She had no idea that everything that happened to her in her lifetime was used by God "for such a time as this."

That's the way we like to believe it happened. But when Mordecai speaks to Esther he actually says, "Who knows if perhaps you were made queen for such a time as this?"

"Who knows if" — there is doubt and there is guesswork in this phrase. Esther had an opportunity to save the world or save herself in this moment. She had to believe that God had been working all things in her life for good.

Who knows if God has brought you to where you are today just so you can step into your purpose and His plan? Who knows if you are primed and ready to make a difference at this exact moment? Who knows if this situation you are in — this situation that might not be very pleasant — is exactly where you need to be for living out your purpose?

What if you believed Romans 8:2: "And we know that God causes everything to work together for the good of those who love God and are called according to his purpose for them" (NLT).

Esther doesn't go through it alone, does she?

Read Esther 4:15-17

What did Esther ask of Mordecai?

Esther called on everyone she knew and trusted and asked them to seek God on her behalf. Then and only then did she go to King Xerxes on the third day of the fast.

When was the last time you prayed and asked God what your purpose is?

When was the last time you asked others to pray with you about your purpose?

If you have never asked God what purpose He has planned for your life, now is the time to do it.

Write out your request to God. Be honest and sincere. Don't worry about grammar or prayer structure. Don't worry about offending God. Communicate with Him as if you are communicating with a friend.

If Esther had chosen to save her own life, God may have found another way to save His people. But that wasn't His plan. His plan was for her to trust Him, step into her purpose, and save His people. Esther was the plan.

You are the plan!! You were created on purpose. You were created with a purpose that was knitted into the fabric of your being when God created you.

The enemy might be disguising your purpose with obstacles, pain, hurt, discouragement, and injustice. But God wants you to see His plan and His purpose for your life.

He wants you to be secure in the truth that God has brought you into this world for a purpose and knowing what your purpose is isn't as important as knowing you have one. When the time is right, God will reveal your purpose. Your responsibility is to trust that God is working His plan in your life, even if you don't see it.

drowned out purpose

Moses, Gideon, and Jonah

"And we know that God causes everything to work together for the good of those who love God <u>and are called according to **His** purpose for them</u>" (Romans 8:28 NLT).

We have learned that God can — and will — take the entirety of your past and present and work it together for your good and His purpose.

Share with the group how God has used some difficulty in your life and turned it around for your good and His purpose.

This week, we will be talking about Drowned Out Purpose. Sometimes we are exactly where we need to be to fulfill our purpose; we are poised to step into the plan God has laid out for us. The conditions are perfect, but, for whatever reason, we are completely blind and deaf to God's plan and our purpose. Sometimes we can think of a million reasons why we are not equipped or qualified for our purpose. We allow the voice of the enemy to drown out the voice of God.

The negative voices in Moses', Gideon's, and Jonah's heads were loud. Their doubts, their fears, their shortcomings, their sins, and their mistakes drowned out the voice of God. We will read about their arguments with God. ARGUMENTS WITH GOD! They actually argued with God about their purposes!

Have you ever argued with God about your purpose? Why?

Moses, Gideon, and Jonah feared their purposes. Do you fear your purpose? Why?

Moses feared his purpose. He argued with God, he pleaded with God, he threw out excuses, and he complained. But God knew what Moses was created to do, and nothing — not even Moses — was going to get in the way of God's plan.

Gideon doubted God. He asked God to prove himself THREE times before he accepted God's purpose for his life.

Jonah was full of anger, bitterness, and self-righteousness. He ran from his purpose and from God.

Throughout the Bible, we see different versions of this same story over and over. There is an enemy who desires to hide, disguise, or thwart the purpose of God's people. But God is so much bigger than that. Each and every time He intervenes and turns His people around so they can fulfill His purpose.

In these stories, we see how the strong emotions of doubt and fear can drown out the voice of God. Moses, Gideon, and Jonah just could not seem to look back and see that God had strategically brought them to a place of purpose. All they could see is that they had been brought to a place of brokenness.

In the days to come, we will see how God had His hand on the lives of Moses, Gideon, and Jonah. He was the protector of their past, present, and future. He turned the bad in their lives around for good. His purpose for their lives was fulfilled just as He planned.

God has His hand on your life too. He has a future planned and has had a specific purpose for your life since the beginning of time. Yet, when we are faced with purpose — true, God-given purpose — the voice of our pasts or our presents can drown out the voice of God.

What is drowning out the voice of God in your life?

What is drowning out your purpose?

Jeremiah 29:11 says, "For I know the plans **I** have for you says the Lord …"

He knows about the plans He has for you, but you have a choice. You can deny him the privilege of working His plan through you, and you can allow the enemy to drown out the voice and purpose of God. Or you can step into your purpose and allow the voice of God to drown out the voice of the enemy. He will not force you to say yes. He will not force you to accept His plan. He wants you to willingly step into your purpose, and He wants you to willingly accept His plan.

Are you willing to accept your purpose? No matter what it is? Does it scare you to say yes when you don't know what the future might hold?

His plan is to give you hope and an amazing future full of purpose. What is your plan?

Moses didn't have a plan of his own, but we will find out that he wasn't happy about God's plan either. Moses almost allowed his own self-doubt to drown out the voice of God, but God did not give up on Moses.

Gideon doubted God and tested God, but God did not give up on Gideon. Gideon conquered the enemy and fulfilled a promise God made to His people.

Jonah disagreed with God and then ran from Him. He allowed his own prejudice and self-righteousness to drown out the plan God had for him. But God didn't give up on Jonah. God turned Jonah around and used the shouts of one man to turn a whole city back to God.

God did not give up on Moses or Gideon or Jonah, and God hasn't given up on you.

Even if your purpose has been drowned out by the voices of insecurity, shame, fear, pain, or sin, your purpose is not erased. Your purpose is waiting for you. God is waiting for you to hear His voice and trust in Him. He will bring your purpose to light and fulfill His purpose through you in a way only He can.

disguised purpose

Moses

The Bible tells us that Moses' life was in danger from the very start. Pharaoh had ordered all the baby boys to be thrown into the river to drown, but God had a different plan. Instead of being thrown into the river, Moses was put into a basket by his mom and sent down river. God safely guided Moses' little basket straight to the Pharaoh's daughter. God spared Moses' life, and Moses went on to live a great life — the kind of life that only an adopted son of a princess can live.

If the story was to end here, we would all believe that Moses was set up for success. Moses should be poised to step into his purpose with ease. But in the next chapter of Moses' story, Moses commits a murder. Yes, the man who saved God's people was a murderer.

Read Exodus 2:11-14.

Moses was a murderer and a fugitive, and yet became one of the most famous men of all time. Moses' life and purpose were just getting started, but first he had to have an encounter with God.

Read Exodus 3:7-10. Write down verse 10.

The Lord says, "Now, go. I am sending you." Your purpose belongs to God. It is not for you to decide when and where you will step into it nor is it up to you to determine how you will fulfill it. Your purpose is yours because God gave it to you, and your purpose will be fulfilled according to God's plan. When it is just the right time, He will send you. He will tell you, "Now, go!"

Do you believe God is sending you? Do you want to "go"?

God tells Moses to *go now*. Even though His instructions are perfectly clear, Moses still puts on the brakes. The next words out of Moses' mouth are "Who am I?"

Read Exodus 3:10-13.

How many times did Moses protest?

What were Moses' concerns?

Moses was full of self-doubt. He was hiding, not because he wanted to, but because he had to. And now God was telling him to return to the very place he fled, to return to the people he was hiding from, to return in spite of serious danger.

Do you allow the voice of insecurity, self-doubt, shame, fear, pain, or sin to drown out the voice of God? Do you allow your past or present to rob you of your purpose? Do you argue with God's plan because it will take you back to the place from which you ran?

Moses steps his argument up a notch in Exodus 4:1 NLT: "But Moses protested again, 'What if they won't believe me or listen to me? What if they say, 'The Lord never appeared to you'?"

Here, Moses projects his own doubt on to others. He is so concerned about the thoughts of others that he can't hear the words of God. He is literally arguing with God about whether or not people will believe him. But God is patient. Time and time again He comes up with a solution. Yet, it seems like for every solution God gives, Moses has another concern.

Moses has one last argument and one last insecurity to present to God, and Moses really hopes this last argument will disqualify him for good this time.

Read Exodus 4:10-14

God assures Moses that He will be with him. God tells Moses exactly what to say. But Moses still doesn't trust God. In verse 13, Moses says, "Lord please! Send anyone else."

Moses did not want to step into his purpose. He did not want to be the mouthpiece of God. Moses was so focused on his doubts and the possible doubts of others that he couldn't hear the assurances of God. Moses chose not to hear the plan God had. He allowed the enemy to drown out every word, every solution, every promise, and every miracle God was providing.

How many times do you think you have allowed the words in your head to drown out the words of God? Why do you allow the words in your mind to drown out the words of God?

Moses tried talking God out of the whole plan. Moses tried to convince God that his purpose did not involve leaving his comfort zone. *Moses would have been completely content with having a relationship with God, talking to God, and knowing God without doing anything for God.*

Read Exodus 4:14-16

Moses made God angry! Can you imagine God telling you he's angry with you?

God doesn't show us His anger. However, every time you make an excuse, reject His plan, and deny your purpose, you make God sad and mad. God wants us to bury the words of the enemy with His words. He wants us to bury our self-doubt with his confidence. He wants us to bury our fears with His courage.

Exodus 3:10 – "Now go, for I am sending you…"
Exodus 3:12 – God answered, "I will be with you…"
Exodus 4:12 – "Now go! I will be with you as you speak, and I will instruct you in what to say."

Let these words drown out the voice in your mind, let His promise to never leave you ring in your ears, and let the words that He has a plan and a purpose for you penetrate your heart.

_____ (insert your name) Now go, for I am sending you!

_____ (insert your name) I will be with you!

disguised purpose

Gideon

Gideon, hero of the Old Testament, mighty warrior, leader of a nation, and a man chosen by God. This is how we remember him, but how did he see himself? I'll give you the quick answer: NONE OF THE ABOVE!

As far as Gideon was concerned, he was a nobody. He considered himself insignificant, he lacked courage, and he had a mistrust of God and His promises to the Israelite people.

God, on the other hand, saw Gideon as a man with a purpose, and He was ready to reveal to Gideon exactly what He thought about him.

Read Judges 6:7-12

What did the angel of the Lord call Gideon?

Read Judges 6:13

What was Gideon's immediate response to the angel's words?

Gideon was called a "mighty hero" by an angel of the Lord, and Gideon's immediate response included a scolding and a questioning of God's ways.

God trusted in Gideon a whole lot more than Gideon trusted in God. Gideon had mistrust and bitterness in his heart, and not even the words of God calling him out of his mundane life was enough to inspire him. Instead he criticized God. He was mad and bitter about his life and the lives of the people around him.

God told Gideon, *"I have something for you to do, I have a plan and you are about to fulfill your purpose."* And Gideon responded, *"Then why did you allow bad things to happen to me, my family, and my people? If you are so good, why did bad things happen?"*

Do you ever respond to God's purpose for your life with a question of *why did you allow* **＿＿＿＿＿＿＿** *to happen***? What has happened in your life that has caused you to ask, "Why?"**

As Gideon asked these questions, God was thinking, *"You see the problem, but I see the solution in you."* Gideon couldn't see it. He had buried hope and trust deep under layers of mistrust and bitterness. Because of Gideon's self-doubt, he couldn't see that God planned on him to become the solution.

God was not deterred by Gideon's question. His response was simple.

"Then the LORD turned to him and said, 'Go with the strength you have, and rescue Israel from the Midianites. I am sending you" (Judges 6:14 NLT).

God knew how Gideon would respond, so He preempted all Gideon's doubts before he even voiced them. You would think Gideon's next words would be ones of surrender and obedience. After all, God told him, "GO, with the strength you have right now." *Who you are is enough, what I need is no more and no less than who you are right now. Listen carefully: I am sending you! Go!*

That's pretty clear, right? Not to Gideon! His purpose was staring him in the face, but somehow he found a way to bury it under a few more doubts and insecurities.

Read Judges 6:15

What were Gideon's excuses?

Did God answer his doubts before Gideon voiced them? Was Gideon listening?

What are your doubts?

I love how God continues to build Gideon up. He doesn't get into an argument or go on the defensive — God does not feel the need to explain Himself. God put Gideon on this earth for this purpose. Gideon, on the other hand, is concerned about everything except his purpose. Gideon wants God to explain himself.

Read Judges 6:16

Again, God reassures Gideon that he is the man, he is chosen, he is called, and he will be equipped.

God has chosen YOU, God has called YOU, God is sending YOU and God will equip YOU!

Do you believe God? Do you want to believe God?

Gideon knew these things about God, but he had trust issues. His purpose could have been drowned out by mistrust if he hadn't pursued God and allowed God to see it and fix it.

Read Judges 6:17-21, 36-40

How many times did he test God?

How many times did God prove Himself?

God believes in you. He is patient with your mistrust, He is patient with your self-doubt, and He is patient with your hesitation because you and your purpose are that important.

Gideon went on to do all that God told him he would do, and God did for Gideon all He said he would do.

What is drowning out your purpose? Is it mistrust, self-doubt, hurt, bitterness, or anger? Explain.

God can reveal your purpose if you are willing to dig up and give up _____ .

"Go, with the strength you have right now." Who you are right now is enough; you are precisely what I need, no more and no less than you are right now. Listen carefully: I am sending you! Go!

disguised purpose

Jonah

Jonah, Jonah, Jonah. I shake my head in disappointment as I say his name as if he is the only person who has ever disobeyed and run — yes, I said run — from God.

Jonah was a prophet, and, as far as he was concerned, he had already stepped into his purpose. How much more purpose can you have when you are already a prophet of God, right?

Jonah's story starts with God telling him to "get up and go."

Read Jonah 1:1,2

Jonah was being sent to Nineveh. Some of the most wicked people lived in Nineveh. They were known for their cruelty, idolatry, prostitution, witchcraft, exploitation of the helpless … the list goes on. God saw this wickedness and wanted to warn the people of Nineveh that He was about to destroy them if they didn't repent and turn from their wicked ways.

Jonah had a purpose within his purpose. He was told to GO and warn the people of Nineveh of their impending doom and to tell them to repent. Jonah was comfortable with telling rulers and kings of impending doom. He was used to relaying God's messages, no matter how small or large, so going to Nineveh was no big deal. Except that it was. Jonah didn't want to go. He buried his purpose under anger and self-righteousness and disobedience. Jonah did what Jonah thought he had to do to escape his purpose.

Read Jonah 1:3

What did Jonah do to escape his purpose?

Jonah ran! Not because he didn't understand his purpose, not because he was afraid, not because he didn't love God, not because he didn't trust God, and certainly not because he didn't understand what God was asking him to do. He ran because he didn't want to do what God asked him to do.

Have you ever run from what God has asked you to do? What have you run from?

Jonah hops on a boat and heads in the opposite direction of Nineveh. He didn't just disobey; he ran in the opposite direction. Jonah was burying his purpose deep, and consequently he got buried deep ... in the belly of a fish.

Read Jonah 1:17

Read Jonah Chapter 2

Jonah comes to his senses and vows to fulfill his purpose, so the fish spits him out on a beach. God meets Jonah there on the beach to remind him to go to Nineveh (just in case he had forgotten).

The Lord spoke a second time and said, "Get up and go to the great city of Nineveh, and deliver the message I have given you." Verse three of Chapter Three says, "This time Jonah obeyed the Lord's command." Jonah obeyed, but he wasn't happy about it. Even though he accepted his purpose, he still didn't accept why it was his purpose. Jonah didn't believe the people of Nineveh deserved the warning; he didn't believe they deserved God's grace. Jonah set himself up as the judge of Nineveh, and he condemned them.

Sometimes stepping into your purpose involves stepping back into a situation that hurt you or reentering the life of someone who did you wrong. Sometimes God's purpose for your life may pull you in a direction opposite the one you wish to go.

Which of the two is more important to you? Fulfilling your God-given purpose or liking your purpose?

Sometimes your purpose might bring you into contact with your enemy. Sometimes God is going to use you to reach out to people you don't believe in. Sometimes you will be told "go" to the very place you wish to avoid. Sometimes you won't want to do what is required to fulfill your purpose

Are you willing to go to the place you hope to avoid to fulfill your purpose in God's plan?

Are you willing to be uncomfortable for the sake of obedience to God?

Read Jonah 3:4,5

Jonah shouted to the crowds. That's a halfhearted try if I ever heard one. Jonah was in a city of 120,000 people, and he shouted the message God gave him. How many people do you think heard him? He was the ONLY messenger God sent to warn these people that they are headed for destruction, and Jonah decided to shout the warning in the midst of a crowd of people.

God took Jonah's half-hearted attempt and did what only He can do: He changed the hearts of the people, and the people of Nineveh repented and turned to God.

Jonah wasn't happy about it though. Jonah wanted God to punish the people of Nineveh. Jonah wanted God to destroy them. All the wisdom Jonah could have gained from fulfilling his purpose was drowned out by anger, bitterness, and self-righteousness even after he fulfilled his purpose.

Because Jonah was so focused on his own wants, he missed out on the lesson and the joy of his purpose. He missed out on the high-five with God, he missed out on the miracle of lives changed, and he missed out on the thrill of a purpose fulfilled.

Your purpose is a gift from God. Fulfilling your purpose will bless your life, bless the lives of others, and will put a smile on Jesus' face. Don't allow your purpose to be drowned out by anger or bitterness. Embrace the journey of your purpose.

Write a prayer of surrender to God. Write in detail your feelings and fears, hesitations and oppositions, concerns and worries, and be honest about what is drowning out your purpose.

revealed purpose

ordinary purpose

Nobody wants to be called ordinary; nobody strives to be ordinary. Yet most of us would consider our lives to be ordinary. Most of us do ordinary things in the course of our ordinary days which causes our lives to become ordinary. It makes sense that we would see ourselves as ordinary.

Our culture tells us that ordinary is a bad thing, that everyday, ordinary things are useless in a world that strives to be bigger and better. Should we believe this? Is bigger also better? Is ordinary synonymous with failure?

In what ways do you consider yourself ordinary?

Don't discount your ordinary! In fact, embrace it! This week, we are going to learn about ordinary people of the Bible and how God <u>needed</u> their ordinary, everyday lives to do something extraordinary.

List a few ordinary, everyday things that impact the people around you in an extraordinary way.

Write down Matthew 10:42

Giving a cup of water to a stranger is an ordinary act, but giving a cup of water on Jesus' behalf makes the act extraordinary. There is no such thing as an ordinary act, there is no such thing as an ordinary life, and there is no such thing as an ordinary purpose IF our actions, lives, and purposes are carried out on Jesus behalf.

The enemy wants us to believe that we can't make a difference. Or that our purpose must be showcased on the world's stage to be worth anything. But all Jesus wants from us is a willingness to step into the purpose He gives us to be blessed and multiplied.

When we compare ourselves to God, we are ordinary. But God doesn't compare Himself to us because there is no comparison. He looks at us as His kids. We are the loves of His life. He wants good things and God things for us, and when He looks at us, He doesn't see ordinary. He sees a masterpiece created on purpose with a purpose.

God doesn't see you as ordinary, so why do you?

We have to change our way of thinking. Our battle with being ordinary exists in our minds — it is won there, and it is lost there. In the next three studies, we will watch Sarah, Moses, and Gideon argue with God because what they thought about themselves did not match up with what God thought about them.

Find a scripture that describes what God thinks about you and write it down.

Does that match up with what you think about yourself?

There is no such thing as an ordinary creation by God.
There is no such thing as an ordinary act of God.
There is no such thing as an ordinary purpose from God.

If you believe that you have a God-given purpose, then you believe you have an extraordinary purpose and that God is going to use that purpose in an extraordinary way. You don't get to call yourself a child of God who was formed in your mother's womb with a God-given purpose, and then, in the same breath, call yourself and your purpose ordinary. You don't get to tell God that His masterpiece is average. You don't get to tell God that His plan for your life in not big enough.

Here is what you get to say…

Psalm 139:13-16 NLT
You made all the delicate, inner parts of my body
and knit me together in my mother's womb.
Thank you for making me so wonderfully complex!
Your workmanship is marvelous—how well I know it.
You watched me as I was being formed in utter seclusion,
as I was woven together in the dark of the womb.
You saw me before I was born.
Every day of my life was recorded in your book.
Every moment was laid out
before a single day had passed.

How precious are your thoughts about me, O God.
They cannot be numbered!

I can't even count them;
  they outnumber the grains of sand!
And when I wake up,
  you are still with me!

God is so good; He takes your purpose, blesses it, and multiplies it. That makes it so much more than ordinary — it makes your purpose extraordinary.

ordinary purpose

Five Loaves & Two Fish

Nobody wants his or her purpose to be ordinary. Nobody wants the world at large to regard his or her purpose as ordinary. We all want to know that we have a place in this world, that what we do will make a difference, and that we will be remembered.

What purpose would you view as ordinary?

What purpose would you view as extraordinary?

Today we will read about a boy who isn't even given a name in these scriptures. And then you will decide if his purpose was ordinary or extraordinary.

Read John 6:1-10

How many people did Jesus need to feed?

Who supplied the five loaves and two fish?

Jesus is obviously the miracle worker in this story. He took five loaves of bread and two fish, and He fed five thousand men, plus women and children. There is nothing ordinary about that! I think we can all agree that Jesus is truly extraordinary.

But what about the "young boy"? He played a significant role in this miracle, didn't he? Here is what we know: He was there to listen to Jesus, and he had food. He wasn't heroic or brave. He didn't have the weight of the world on his shoulders. He wasn't asked to free an enslaved people. He was simply there to listen to Jesus ... and he happened to have five loaves of bread and two fish.

His role in the miracle began with giving all he had, even though he didn't know what Jesus was about to do with it. He was the only person there with food, so he could have sold it or he could have eaten it. But he didn't. He gave it away — he gave it to Jesus.

What did Jesus disciples say in John 6:9? Write it down.

Five loaves and two fish. "What good is that with this huge crowd?" (NLT) Those words came out of the mouths of Jesus' disciples. The very same disciples who watched as Jesus performed miracle after miracle; the men with extraordinary purposes; the friends who spent time learning from Jesus, following Him, loving Him, and believing in Him.

They couldn't see what Jesus could do with five loaves and two fish. The "young boy" who gave up all he had didn't question Jesus. It's as if he said, *"Let's see how much good He can do with this."*

What are you saying to Jesus? Are you asking, "What good is my purpose in this world?" Or, are you declaring, "I can't wait to see how much good you can do with my purpose in this world!"

Jesus took those five loaves and two fish and He blessed them. He combined His extraordinary power with the young boy's ordinary offering, and He multiplied it. He multiplied it until there was so much left over the disciples had to gather up twelve baskets' worth.

The "young boy" had the ordinary purpose of bringing five loaves and two fish to a hillside revival with Jesus. He stepped into his purpose by giving it all to Jesus.

You may feel ordinary like the nameless boy. You may feel that the metaphorical bread and fish you offer to the world is not enough. After all, you know you don't have the power to multiply your purpose.

But Jesus does.

What if you gave those five loaves and two fish to Jesus? What if you gave all the purpose you have to Jesus and what if you let him bless and multiply your purpose?

That is what the young boy did; he gave what he had to Jesus. I wonder what it felt like to sit among the crowd watching them eat until they were full, knowing that all those people were fed. They were not fed because the boy had enough, but because Jesus made what the boy had enough.

Gideon didn't think he was enough. He referred to his family as the weakest in the whole tribe and then to himself as the "least" in his family. He said he was the lowest of the low. And this is how God responded:

"Then the LORD turned to him and said, "Go with the strength you have, and rescue Israel from the Midianites. I am sending you" (Judges 6:15 NLT).

God doesn't rate our purpose as non-existent, ordinary, or extraordinary — but He does evaluate our obedience that way.

How would God rate your obedience?

Your purpose is better in the hands of Jesus than it is in your hands. Don't worry about labeling your purpose. Instead, put your ordinary purpose in the hands of Jesus and know that He will make it enough, He will bless it, and He will multiply it.

GO, with the strength _____ (insert your name) has right now, who _____ (insert your name) is right now is enough, no more and no less than _____ (insert your name) is right now is who He needs, He will bless and multiply the purpose _____ (insert your name) gives to Him, now listen carefully, He is sending _____ (insert your name), go!

ordinary purpose

Mary

Nobody in their right mind would put Mary's purpose in the "ordinary" category. It almost sounds sacrilegious — she was the mother of Jesus, for crying out loud!

But I bet if we could sit down with Mary and have a conversation, she would tell us that ordinary is exactly what being the mother of Jesus felt like, all the way until His death and resurrection.

Her journey didn't begin in an ordinary way. Mary's story starts with an angel of the Lord filling her in on her role in plans that had already been set in motion. The angel didn't ask for her permission and he didn't ask her how she felt about it. It was her purpose from the beginning of time. She was already chosen.

Read Luke 1:26-38

What did the angel call Mary?

He called her favored, he called her chosen, he called her worthy, he called her special, and he called her to give birth to Jesus. When you were formed in your mother's womb, God wove His purpose into the fabric of your being.

He called you favored, chosen, worthy, special, precious, equipped, protected and loved.

What was Mary's response in verse 38?

Her response was submission, acceptance, and obedience. That is all God wants from us. He wants to hear us say "yes". He wants us to acknowledge that we are here for Him and His plan. He wants to know that we are willing and ready to accomplish our purpose for Him.

Three days later, Mary hurried to see her cousin. Mary may have thought she was going crazy or she may have thought she heard wrong. Perhaps she was afraid or maybe she was excited.

Read Luke 1:39-45

Mary rushed to see her cousin. She barely got a hello out of her mouth, and immediately Elizabeth started to congratulate her. Elizabeth's congratulations were the equivalent of the two little pink lines on a pregnancy test. Mary suddenly knew this was real, she was not crazy, she did not hear wrong, and she would give birth to Jesus. I'm not sure what kind of life she was expecting to live, but as the mother of Jesus, I'm sure she didn't expect it to be ordinary.

I don't know what Mary was feeling at that moment, but Elizabeth speaks the most encouraging words a person in any situation could ever want to hear.

Write down Luke 1:45

Elizabeth could have said Mary was blessed for countless reasons — one of which was that she was carrying the Son of God. Instead, Elizabeth simply said, "You are blessed because you BELIEVED that the Lord would do what He said" (NLT).

I have that verse highlighted in every Bible I own; I have it written on a 3 x 5 card and I have it on my phone. If you believe that the Lord has called you out by name and He has a purpose for your life and you are willing to fulfill anything and everything that He asks of you, you are blessed! No matter what your purpose is, how ordinary you think it is, how difficult it is, or how long it takes to fulfill, you are blessed!

Find a scripture that speaks to His belief in your purpose and write it below.

List seven descriptive words that God would use to describe His purpose for your life.

1.   5.

2.   6.

3.   7.

4.

Mary raised Jesus. She changed His diapers, fed Him, bathed Him, potty-trained Him, took Him to church, walked with Him through puberty, had dreams for Him, and loved Him. Mary lived a very ordinary life! Her extraordinary beginning evolved into an ordinary life of marriage and children.

Sometimes, our purpose looks normal and ordinary. It slips into everyday life, and if we are not careful, we will forget that every day plays a part in our purpose. Every day matters, every day is a stepping stone to the next day, every day is a stepping stone on the path of purpose.

Discouragement may set in as you wait to see God finish what He started in you. Elizabeth put it beautifully: "You are blessed because you *believed* that the Lord would do what He said." God's put your purpose inside of you and

He wants to work His purpose in you every day. It is your job to say "yes" — all day and every day — until He completes his good work in you.

Write down Philippians 1:6

Mary had the privilege to be there the moment her son became her Savior. She watched as He fulfilled His extraordinary purpose. All because she said yes to an ordinary life of purpose.

And I _____ (insert your name) am certain that God, who began the good work within _____ (insert your name), will continue His work until it is finally finished on the day when Christ Jesus returns.

ordinary purpose

The Man Who Carried the Cross

The man who carried the cross was named Simon. He was from Cyrene in North Africa, and he expected this day to be like any other. There was no reason to suspect that this day would change his life forever.

Simon was celebrating the Passover Feast in remembrance of God's deliverance from death during the time of Moses. God promised the Israelite people that the angel of death would pass over every house if they had the blood of a lamb or goat on their doorframe (Exodus 12:23).

To celebrate this festival was to celebrate God's protection and deliverance from slavery. This was a festival you did not miss and you did not take lightly. Simon was ready to eat, remember, and be thankful. Simon had no idea that a man named Jesus had been sentenced to death and was headed down the very same road on which Simon was walking.

Read Matthew 27:26-33

Simon and Jesus had a divine meeting on the road that day. Jesus, in His weakened state, could not take another step. Simon, who was purposed to be there at that very moment, was grabbed by the Roman soldiers and forced to carry Jesus' cross.

> Jesus was weak because He had been beaten so we could be made whole (Isaiah 53:5)

Jesus was weak because He was whipped so we could be healed (Isaiah 53:5)

Jesus was weak because He was paying the price for the sin of the man carrying His cross. Jesus was weak because He wanted the man who was carrying His cross to be healed and made whole. Jesus was on His way to die for the man carrying His cross so the man could spend eternity with Him.

Take a moment to read that again and then let it soak in and penetrate your heart.

Simon, an ordinary man living an ordinary life having an ordinary day, was chosen to have an extraordinary encounter with Jesus — the same Jesus who died for him and saved him.

One moment of purpose can change your life and the lives of those around you forever. One ordinary day can be the day you have an encounter with Jesus that turns your ordinary into extraordinary.

Simon may not have known he was having an encounter with Jesus. Simon may not have known whose cross he was carrying — and he may not have cared. But he did it anyway. He carried the cross of a broken and beaten man, a man who was condemned to die. Simon was there when he was needed, and he fulfilled a purpose he didn't even know he had.

The Bible says Simon was "forced" to carry Jesus' cross for Him. Simon almost missed out on helping his Savior, and he almost missed out on fulfilling his purpose.

How many times have you come across someone in need and you decided not to help him or her?

How many times did you feel an urge to do something but you chose not to? What was it? Why did you choose not to?

Ordinary purpose comes along when there is an ordinary need, and when you meet that need something amazing happens. God puts His touch on your ordinary obedience. He reveals it as purpose, then makes your ordinary purpose extraordinary!

Next time you come across an ordinary need, what are you going to do? Why?

Write down a scripture that affirms your "why".

So many times, we struggle to find our purpose, and so many times, we are looking directly at it but are unwilling to see it. We expect our purpose to save the world, but all we need to do is introduce the world to our Savior by being the hands and feet of Jesus.

Write down Mark 10:45

Simon was Jesus' hands and feet. Simon carried the cross for Jesus, and he served the Savior. Now it is our turn to be the hands and feet for Jesus and to serve for our Savior. One of the greatest purposes we will ever have is to serve our Savior and serve for our Savior.

Simon got one verse in the book of Matthew, a small detail in the grand story of Jesus. But to Simon it wasn't a small detail, it was a purpose lived out.

You may get one small line in the history of our world, but to God and to you, it is not a small line at all. It is a life of purpose lived out, a life of significance, a moment in history that changed you and the world around you forever,

What if the one verse you got in life looked like this:

Along the way, they came across _____ (insert your name) and _____ (insert your name) gladly carried the burden of _____ .

That would look like a life full of extraordinary purpose.

extraordinary purpose

Noah built an ark.
Moses freed Israel from slavery.
David killed the giant.
Esther saved her people from annihilation.
Mary gave birth to Jesus.
Jesus died for our sins.

Yup, I think all the big, heroic, and extraordinary purposes are already taken. Now that our expectation of saving the world with our purpose is gone, we can talk realistically.

God doesn't need us to save the world, He doesn't need us to fix or free people, He doesn't need us to be heroes. <u>He needs us to need Him</u> so He can do amazing and extraordinary things through us.

Someone once asked a pastor why God allows sinners to lead churches. The pastor answered her with a question of his own: "Who else does He have to use? We are all sinners."

God uses willing and obedient people to do extraordinary things. He uses our limited ability to highlight His extraordinary ability. Every single one of us is a sinner in need of a Savior. We are powerless to change the world unless He is changing it through us.

It is a privilege to be given a purpose by God. Why He chose to work through us, I don't know. But He chose us.

Write down John 15:16

He chose us! He chose you!

What did He appoint you to do in John 15:16?

He chose and appointed you to "**go** and bear fruit — fruit that will last." He wants us to go, and he wants us to grow. "Fruit that will last" is purpose-given, blessed and multiplied by God, and accepted by us.

We all want to leave a legacy and do something that will outlive us. This is the way to do it. *Purpose is about giving, not taking; it's about going, not staying; it's about growing, not dying; and it's about giving away, not hoarding.*

Sum up in three words what purpose is about.

1.

2.

3.

If I had to sum it up in my own words I would say: Go, Grow, Give Away.

How can you go?

How do you grow?

How do you give away?

God didn't just save you from something, He saved you *for* something!

What have you been saved from?

What have you been saved for?

Jesus knew who He was saving, why He needed to save us, and who He was saving us from.

Write down John 10:10

This was Jesus' purpose. We were Jesus' purpose. He accomplished His purpose by dying on the cross so we could have life. Not just any life, an abundant life full of extraordinary purpose.

He did His part, so now it is our turn to do our part. His purpose was to give us life, so now it is our turn to live that life. It is our turn to live all that

God planned for us and live out every purpose to its fullest. It is our turn to **go**, **grow**, and **give it away!**

Write down Luke 6:38

I like the NLT version of this scripture: "Give, and you will receive. Your gift will return to you in full — pressed down, shaken together to make room for more, running over, and poured into your lap. The amount you give will determine the amount you get back."

When we go, grow, and give away, we don't lose anything. In fact, Jesus says "give, and you will receive." But my favorite part is, "the amount you give will determine the amount you get back."

This is a reminder that we are to give first. When we give, we let Jesus bless our offering and multiply it so much that it "will return to you in full — pressed down, shaken together to make room for more, running over, and poured into your lap."

God's gift to you is purpose, and your gift to God is using it. But God will not be outdone. He promises to give you even more than you can handle just because you honored Him with obedience and you blessed others with your purpose.

When is God honored?

So go, embrace your purpose, and give it away!

extraordinary purpose

Jesus

Jesus became the solution for all sin the moment Eve committed the first sin. His purpose came about through her disobedience. I would love to blame it all on Eve, but that wouldn't be fair. Since the fall of man, every single one of us has kept up the tradition of sinning with no sign of slowing down.

Jesus' purpose was to be born on this earth, live on this earth, and then to die on this earth for everyone who would ever live on this earth.

Write down Isaiah 53:5 NLT

"He personally carried our sins in his body on the cross so that we can be dead to sin and live for what is right. By His wounds you are healed" (I Peter 2:24 NLT).

This is His story. **We were His purpose**, and this was His calling. His purpose was to "go," just like it was for Moses, Gideon, and Jonah. Just like them, He knew the cost, so He prayed three times for God to spare Him the pain of His purpose.

Read Matthew 26:37-44

Unlike Moses, Gideon, and Jonah, Jesus didn't run, didn't argue, didn't try to strike a deal, and didn't beg for someone else to take His place. He didn't doubt himself and He didn't doubt God. He took His request and concerns to God, and when the answer was clear that this was His purpose, He trusted God and He obeyed.

Write down Matthew 26:39

"... I want *your will* to be done, *not mine*" (NLT). Nine simple words that changed the world. Nine words that changed your world.

We were created with a purpose and for a purpose, but it is up to us to accept it and step into it. We can pray, we can beg, we can ask God to send someone else, but at the end of your prayer the correct response should always be:

_____ .

Jesus walked this earth so He could save the earth. Even though He was dismissed, belittled, tempted, mocked, falsely accused, talked about, and lied about, He knew that His purpose was too important to allow any of that to discourage Him.

His purpose was to save the world so that through our purpose we can bring people to the Savior of the world. God didn't just save you from something, He saved you FOR something. He saved you so you could live out your purpose.

God wants to know that the purpose He has for your life is just as important to you as it is to Him.

The question is, IS IT? Is your purpose just as important to you as it is to God? Explain why.

We have one great commission — one great purpose — which is to **"go"**.

> "And then he told them, "Go into all the world and preach the Good News to everyone" (Mark 16:15 NLT).

> "Therefore, go and make disciples of all the nations, baptizing them in the name of the Father and the Son and the Holy Spirit" (Matthew 28:19 NLT).

We are all purposed to do this in the way God designed us to do it. Some will "go into all the world" via the World Wide Web and social media. Others will literally go into all the physical world.

Some of us will "go" by giving a cup of water in Jesus' name or bringing five loaves and two fish to be blessed and multiplied. You may be chosen to care for and help carry the burdens of others just like Simon carried Jesus' burden when he could no longer carry the cross.

What can you do? Write down the first thing that pops into your mind. No matter what it is.

Jesus took His purpose to "go" to the cross seriously. It wasn't an easy choice. He gave up His life, but He gained it back. His loss was temporary. He rose from the dead and He gave us eternal life because of His obedience when God told Him to "go.'

Now it is your turn!

"Go, with the strength you have right now." Who you are right now is enough; you are precisely what God needs, no more and no less than you are right now. Listen carefully: He is sending you! Go!

extraordinary purpose

You

God didn't just save you from something, He saved you *for* something!

God didn't just save _____ (insert your name) from something,
He saved _____ (insert your name) *for* something.

We have learned about many people in the Bible who had a God-given purpose. Some of them embraced it, while others argued with God. One of them even ran from God. But, time and time again, we saw the patience and grace of God displayed, not because we are good, but because He is good.

What was the common theme of all the stories we read?

God wanted them to "go," and they didn't want to! Sounds a little like us, doesn't it? God wants us to "go," but we don't want to. We want our purpose, but we don't want the responsibility. Our ordinary purpose becomes extraordinary the minute we "go." His plan depends on our willingness to "go."

The purpose God has given you is always just a hop and a skip of obedience away. He gladly takes that obedience and turns it into purpose. He then blesses it, multiplies it, and turns it into extraordinary purpose.

Obedience doesn't mean we lack plans for our lives; it means we are okay with letting go of our plans when God has a different plan.

Write down Proverbs 16:9

Write down Proverbs 19:21

Over and over again you read that God has a plan and He has a purpose for your life. Over and over again you read that your purpose is in the hands of God. Over and over again you read that He will lead you right to it. God will put your purpose on your path, directly in your way, and He will ask you to abandon your plans and to accept His plan.

Our job is to *trust* Him, to believe that He will do what He says He will do. Then we are to do what He tells us to do. That is a whole lot of active "doing" in living out our purposes, but that is what purpose is all about. It is all about obeying when He says "go" and "do."

Write down Proverbs 3:5-6

If we delay obedience until we understand what God is trying to do, we will never do a single thing for God. Purpose is not about understanding. It is about trust and obedience. The "young boy" with the five loaves and two fish didn't ask questions. He obeyed, then waited to see what God was going to do with his offering.

Write down Psalm 119:105

Not only will God guide your steps, He will light up your path as well. If you are following God, He will lead you to your purpose every time. Most people spend the majority of their days chasing their purpose, when all God wants you to do is follow Him to your purpose.

You will never find your God-given purpose away from God — you will never find it all by yourself and nobody can find it for you. Only God knows what your purpose is, where your purpose fits into His plan, and when He will reveal your purpose to you.

Will you stop chasing your purpose? Will you start following God to your purpose?

Write a prayer of submission to God's plan and path.

Your purpose is extraordinary because our God is extraordinary. Your influence is great because our God is all-powerful. Your voice will be heard because it is God speaking through you. The difference you make will be great because it is God making the difference. Our world will be changed because God will change it through you. Your purpose is extraordinary because our God is extraordinary!

"Go, with the strength you have right now." Who you are right now is enough; you are precisely what God needs, no more and no less than you are right now. Listen carefully: He is sending you! Go!

extraordinary purpose

Purpose

Our first and most important step to our purpose is to have an encounter with Jesus. We must meet Him at the cross, accept what He has done for us, repent for what we have done to Him, and then to love Him and live for Him. Because of His extraordinary sacrifice, His extraordinary love, and His extraordinary grace, we can now live extraordinary lives.

Purpose is one of the most intangible things we seek. Wouldn't it be easier if God took us straight to purpose rather than God taking us through purpose?

But that would rob us of the journey to purpose. The journey to purpose is a refining tool, an action tool, an obedience tool, and a growth tool. Purpose is in us to be used through us for the benefit of others and for God's glory. That is the purpose of purpose. Even purpose has a purpose.

Read Matthew 28:18-20

"… and be sure of this; I am with you always even to the end of the age" (Matthew 28:20 NLT).

"Do not be afraid or discouraged, for the LORD will personally go ahead of you. He will be with you; He will neither fail you nor abandon you" (Deuteronomy 31:8 NLT).

When God tells you to go, He goes with you! The journey to and through purpose is not something you do alone. Purpose is given to you by God and you are accompanied by God. He goes with you! He lights the path, He guides your steps, He leads you, and He directs you.

When we allow God to light our paths, lead the way, and direct us, we are following in the footsteps of Jesus. Jesus gave it all. His purpose was to give His life for us. His sacrifice leads me to believe that when we step into our purpose we will be called to give something away. Life will no longer be about ourselves, but about the message of Jesus. We will give cups of water in His name; we will sacrifice of our pride, insecurities, selfishness, and comfort for the greater good; we will accept God's best for our lives and the lives around us.

At the end of the day, your purpose is not meant to change your life even though the process will be life-changing. Your purpose is designed and given to you to change the world for Jesus and turn the world to Jesus. Purpose is not about us. It is not a gift to us, it is a gift God uses through us.

What does that mean to you?

Purpose is an action, not a possession.

What does that mean to you?

Purpose is not to be hoarded, but to be given away.

What does that mean to you?

Purpose is only found in the pursuit of God's heart. When you pursue God, He works in you so He can fulfill His purpose through you.

Write down Philippians 2:13

Our first responsibility is to have a relationship with Jesus. When we allow Him to work in us, He, in turn, will work through us. We spend way too much time pursuing our worth, legacy, and purpose, and not enough time pursuing the One who will give us all we desire and so much more. He accepts what we have, He blesses it, and He multiplies it.

You have an extraordinary purpose, and that purpose will be found in the heart of God.

Write down Jeremiah 29:13

It will be tempting to seek God's heart to find your purpose or to find next steps in your purpose. But don't do it — don't search for your purpose in the heart of God. Instead, search for the heart of God and allow Him to reveal your purpose to you.

We make plans for our lives, and we have an idea of what we want our purpose to be. But if we are seeking our wanted purpose in the heart of God, we may miss His purpose for our lives.

Write down Proverbs 19:21

Write your prayer to this scripture. God, I want ... but I know YOU want ...

Write down Ephesians 2:10

Often, our purpose is drawn out and lived out, embedded in the bustle of our day and lives. Sometimes we can only see our purpose in the rearview mirror. Other times, we see our purpose far off in the distance.

Faith in God's master plan for you will keep you going in the dry seasons, and faith in God's master plan will keep you afloat when rain comes flooding in. If you are unsure what your purpose is — or if you even have one — God assures you that you do have one and it can be found in the heart of God.

"Go, with the strength you have right now." Who you are right now is enough; no more and no less than you are right now is who God needs. Now listen carefully: He is sending you! Go!

celebrating purpose

Let's begin by talking about your exciting, brave, significant, big, spectacular, or extraordinary purpose.

Circle the descriptive word above that best describes your purpose.

> "For we are God's workmanship, created in Christ Jesus to do good works, which God prepared in advance <u>as our way of life</u>" (Ephesians 2:10 BSB).

Read that verse out loud. Now fill in the blanks.

_____ (insert your name) is God's _____ ,
created in Christ Jesus to do _____ .
    God prepared this and _____ (insert your name)
in _____ as _____ (insert your name) way of life.

Isn't it beautiful when you put your name to His promises?

    God thought about you, planned you, and knit you together in your mother's womb. You were fearfully and wonderfully made to change the world around you through the purpose He put inside of you.

> "For I know the plans I have for you," says the LORD. "They are plans for good and not for disaster, to give you a future and a hope" (Jeremiah 29:11 NLT).

God says He knows the plans He has for you and they are good. His plans are for your good.

Fill in the blanks.

For I know that God has plans for _____ (insert your name); they are plans for _____ and not for _____ ; they will be my _____ and they will be full of _____ .

He knows about the plans He has for you, but the choice to accept His plan is yours. You can deny him the privilege of working His plan through you, and you can allow the enemy to drown out the voice and purpose of God. Or you can allow the voice of God to drown out the voice of the enemy. His voice and His words are sweet — sweeter than anything you will ever hear.

God thinks precious thoughts about you — so many precious thoughts that they can't even be counted! They outnumber the grains of sand. When you fall asleep, He is with you; and when you wake up, He is still there.

Psalm 139:13-16 NLT (insert your name):

You made all the delicate, inner parts of _____ body
and knit _____ together in my mother's womb.
Thank you for making _____ so wonderfully complex!
Your workmanship is marvelous — how well I know it.
You watched _____ as I was being formed in utter seclusion,
As _____ was woven together in the dark of the womb.
You saw _____ before I was born.
Every day of _____ life was recorded in your book.
Every moment was laid out
before a single day had passed.

How precious are your thoughts about _____ , O God.
They cannot be numbered!
I can't even count them;
they outnumber the grains of sand!
And when I wake up,
you are still with _____ !

God is with you through it all, and all things work together for good. All things! That means Jesus takes the good and the bad, the hurtful and the painful, the happy and the sad, the devastating and the unforgivable, the grace and the forgiveness, the healing and the restoration. He takes them all and weaves them together for good. He leaves no part of your life untouched. He takes it as a whole and uses it for His purpose and your good.

If you love God, you can't outrun, out-sin, out-hurt, or outlive your purpose. Your purpose is given to you, protected and inspired by God.

Romans 8:28 NLT (insert your name):

And _____ knows that God causes everything to work together for the good of _____ , who loves God and is called according to His purpose for _____ .

God believes in you. He is patient with your hesitation to say yes. He is patient with your mistrust, your self-doubt, and your hesitation because you and your purpose are that important. God sees in you a solution to a problem happening in the world around you.

And He says: Go, with the strength you have right now. Who you are right now is enough; no more and no less than you are right now is who He needs. Now, listen carefully: He is sending you! Go!

Go with the purpose I have given you. Go with the gifts you have to offer. I will bless it and multiply it.

No matter what your purpose is, how ordinary you think your purpose is, how difficult your purpose is, or how long your purpose takes to fulfill, *you are blessed* and your purpose is extraordinary! If you believe that the Lord has called you out by name, that He has a purpose for your life, and you are willing to fulfill anything and everything that He asks of you, *you are blessed* and your purpose is extraordinary!

Philippians 1:6 (insert your name)

And I, _____ , am certain that God, who began the good work within _____ , will continue His work until it is finally finished on the day when Christ Jesus returns.

One moment of purpose can change your life and the lives of those around you forever. One ordinary day can be the day you have an encounter with Jesus that begins your good work. One ordinary moment in one ordinary day can be the time God turns your ordinary into extraordinary.

Jesus made the encounter possible, He made our purpose possible, and His death made our eternity with Him possible.

"But he was pierced for our rebellion, crushed for our sins. He was beaten so we could be whole. He was whipped so we could be healed" (Isaiah 53:5 NLT).

This is His story. **We were His purpose** and He did all of this for us so we would:

"Go into all the world and preach the Good News to everyone" (Mark 16:15 NLT).

You were not just saved from something, you were saved for something!

Purpose is not something you will do alone. Purpose is given to you by God and accompanied by God. He lights the path, He guides your steps, He leads you, and He directs you.

"… And be sure of this; I am with you always even to the end of the age" (Matthew 28:20 NLT).

Most importantly
1. Purpose is not about us; it's not a gift to us, it's a gift God uses through us.
2. Purpose is an action, not a possession.
3. Purpose is not to be hoarded, but to be given away.

True purpose is only found in the pursuit of God's heart. When you pursue God, He works in you so He can fulfill His purpose through you.

You have an extraordinary purpose, and it will be found in the heart of God.

"Go, with the strength you have right now." Who you are right now is enough; you are precisely what God needs, no more and no less than you are right now. Listen carefully: He is sending you! Go!